God, A Mocha & Me

CHIP KAWALSINGH

God, A Mocha & Me contains some of the most profound yet simple keys to living a fruitful life. These are not just good ideas but backed by Scripture. I have known Pastor Chip for many years and he lives what is written in this book. It's not just theory but truth on which you can build a fruitful life, no matter your age.

Dr. Dick Iverson

Chairman of Ministers Fellowship International

There are many books on the market saying many things and for many purposes; some make good reading and some are disappointing. But occasionally a book is written that 'hits the spot'. Chip Kawalsingh's book *God, A Mocha & Me* is a rich diet of Biblical principles. It is full of life's experiences that will help us understand how to walk in wholeness through our Christian lives. Whether it is understanding, church, marriage, attitude, finances or relationships, this book is a rich picking of good seed to sow, not only into our own life but into the lives of others.

A book of refreshing change that does not have theological teaching that no-one understands, but it has theology that relates to life. Once again, a book well written by Chip. Well done and thank you for all your efforts to bless so many.

Pastor Colin Cooper

Leader of Cathedral House, Huddersfield, England
Chairman of Ministers Fellowship Europe

God, a mocha & me

Principles For Highly Successful Living

CHIP KAWALSINGH

www.harvestcitypublishing.com

ISBN 978-0-9561415-0-7
A catalogue record for this book is available from the British Library

First published in the UK in 2009
by Harvest City Publishing

Printed by the MPG Books Group in the UK

Scripture References

Scripture taken from The Message. Copyright © 1993, 1994, 1995, 1996, 2000, 2001, 2002. Used by permission of NavPress Publishing Group.
Scripture quotations marked NLT are taken from the Holy Bible, New Living Translation, copyright 1996, 2004. Used by permission of Tyndale House Publishers, Inc., Wheaton, Illinois 60189. All rights reserved.
Scripture taken from the New King James Version. Copyright © 1982 by Thomas Nelson,Inc. Used by permission. All rights reserved.
Also used is the Contemporary English Version © 1995 by the American Bible Society. Used by permission. All Rights Reserved.
Scripture taken from the HOLY BIBLE, NEW INTERNATIONAL VERSION®. Copyright © 1973, 1978, 1984 International Bible Society. Used by permission of Zondervan. All rights reserved.
Scripture quotations taken from the Amplified® Bible, Copyright © 1954, 1958, 1962, 1964, 1965, 1987 by The Lockman Foundation. Used by permission. (www.Lockman.org)

Emphasis has been added to some scriptures by the author, other personal comments on scripture are in italics.

Acknowledgements

Thanks to the following awesome, dedicated and talented people who worked tirelessly behind the scenes to help make this book possible: Nicky Holmes, Paul Goffin, Darrell Woods and Nick Holmes - CK.

Dedication

I would like to dedicate this book to my Family, my wife Sarah and my two boys, Brandon and Dylan.

To my wife Sarah

I love you and really appreciate all you do for us as a family. You are my pride and joy!

To my sons

I count it an honour to be your Dad and love you both very much. My prayer is that you follow God all the days of your lives.

Thanks boys for making all my dreams come true. I love you.

Contents

Foreword

The wisest man in the Bible, King Solomon, implored his people to "Get wisdom, get understanding. Wisdom is the principal thing; therefore get wisdom" (Proverbs 4:5, 7). He knew that those who see life as God sees it would have the means by which to make right choices in every area of life. Their obedience would honour the Lord and they would become successful.

It is no different today. God is the same "yesterday, today and forever." God's principles are still true several millennia after Solomon wrote under the inspiration of the Holy Spirit and obedience to His ways still bring success. Biblical principles are still relevant to today's lifestyles.

Pastor Chip Kawalsingh has compiled in this one volume a treasure trove of wisdom on a variety of subjects ranging from marriage to finances to valuing the local church. These are not just historical principles. These are truths that weekly flow from Pastor Chip's preaching. He has put these principles to work in his life, his marriage, his family and in his church and has seen success. The people in his growing church, who are living by these principles, have seen marriages restored, finances recovered, and lives rearranged for victory! They are living proof that God's wisdom will always prevail!

My wife and I have known Chip and his wife, Sarah, for many years. We have watched the progress of their lives and seen the good hand of God upon them. You can judge a tree by its fruit and the fruit of Chip Kawalsingh is good.

Chip Kawalsingh

Grab a cup of something, open this book at any chapter and savour the wonderful aroma of wisdom. Then ask the Lord how you can apply that wisdom to your life. It is God's desire to see you fulfil the purpose for which you were created. The principles in these pages will show you the way to achieve a highly successful life in God.

Dr. Wendell Smith

Senior Pastor at The City Church, Seattle
Vice-Chairman of Ministers Fellowship International

Preface

One of the greatest needs of the believer is to spend time with God. It seems that today people all across the world are suffering with less and less time. The average believer today has lost the time when they can pray effectively, when they can read the Word and hear from God about what to do in life. One BBC report says that the average Britain works 36 hours a day, an amazing feat given we only have 24 hours in a day!

Time is becoming scarce. The secret places seem to be locked away. When we do get the time to pray it seems to be brief, at the mercy of the demands of an ever-increasing pace of life. Jesus himself tells us "that my sheep know my voice." Taking time to be with God not only builds us up in faith, but it also ensures the believer gets acquainted with the voice of God. This leads to a clear-cut discernment of who He is and all He stands for, which is celebrated in the local church. The believers' greatest weapon is the ability to hear the voice of God above all other voices, and obey His Word.

God, A Mocha & Me aims to provide a series of short life lessons that help believers everywhere to delve deeply into the word of God on various life issues. Each chapter is on a different topic and stands alone, so feel free to read them in whatever order you wish. They are designed and written specifically to give nourishment, and to build up and deepen faith through God's Word. Jesus Himself overcame the devil by the Word. Having the Word of God inside us helps us to grow and becomes obvious on the outside!

Chip Kawalsingh

This book can be read in your workplace on your coffee break, at lunch time, on a plane, on a train or even during your personal devotions. Sit down, pick a topic and within minutes you will be lost in God's Word and He will begin to speak to you!

I wrote this after working with my own church and seeing many new converts come to Jesus, and counselling many seasoned believers as they walk with God. Both new and seasoned believers have the same question, "How do I grow in the Word when I have no time left in the day?"

God, a Mocha & Me helps the believer access the heart of God through His Word - anytime, anywhere. My prayer is that you as a reader get closer to God, become sensitive to His voice and become a strong and effective believer.

Top Tip:
Enjoy this book with a coffee and a blueberry muffin, no need for the low fat option!

Chip Kawalsingh

Section 1

God

Chapter 1

Extra Shot Of Wisdom Please!

Proverbs 9:1-3 (New Living Translation)
[1]Wisdom has built her house; she has carved its seven columns. [2]She has prepared a great banquet, mixed the wines, and set the table. [3]She has sent her servants to invite everyone to come. She calls out from the heights overlooking the city.

Wisdom is one of those things that we could all do with more of. Not just for challenging activities, but for everyday life. When I think about wisdom I automatically think of Solomon. Solomon was blessed by God with wealth, long life and wisdom beyond all other kings (1 Kings 3:4-13).

Solomon had a heritage of wisdom passed on from his father David. In Proverbs 4:1-9 you can read about this great heritage. Solomon also passed on this wisdom to his son Rehoboam in Proverbs 4:10-25 (you can read about Rehoboam in I Kings 12). Both men saw the great need for an extra shot of wisdom in their families. David didn't always make great decisions and his family was messed up! David killed Uriah who was a loyal man to him and took his wife Bathsheba, who was Solomon's mother. In David's family, his own son Amon raped his half sister Tamar. Then Absalom, David's other son, killed Amon his own brother. If that was not bad enough, Absalom undermined David by trying to take the kingdom from him, and he also slept with his father's concubines on the roof top for all of Israel to see. What a messed up life! You see, we don't need to have a perfect start in life to pass on a heritage of wisdom: all you need to do is to ask the Lord, He gives it liberally!

James 1:5 (New International Version)
⁵If any of you lacks wisdom he should ask God, who gives generously to all without finding fault, and it will be given to him.

God is the key to gaining wisdom and understanding for life's problems. Every bit of wisdom we need for life's problems can be accessed through Jesus. Only He can solve our problems through the help of the Holy Spirit and His Church.

Here are seven pillars to building a house of Wisdom:

1. The Fear of the Lord (Proverbs 9:10).
2. Knowledge and Understanding (Proverbs 18:2).
3. Godly Counsel (Proverbs 4:5; 12:15).
4. Foresight, Vision, Common Sense and Accountability (Proverbs 27:12).
5. Accepting Correction (Proverbs 3:11; 12:1; 19:20; 29:15).
6. Self Discipline (Proverbs 1:1-3).
7. Godly Relationships (Proverbs 11:30).

My To-Do List!

1. I Ask For Wisdom Every Day

If we ask for wisdom above everything else, then God will make sure the things we need will come our way. The key is asking for wisdom. Life is about choices, and we are who we are because of the choices we make in life.

2. Make Good Choices

A good decision can save you time, money and heartache. The opposite will happen with bad decision making - it will cost you! A track record of good choices makes for a blessed and prosperous life. A great saying is "things which matters most should never be at the mercy of things which matter least" - Johann Von Goethe. Putting God and His Kingdom first should never be the least! That is what matters the most! (Matthew 6:33)

3. Be In Church!

When life's challenges come knocking on your door, don't stay at home or have a duvet day, get up and get to church! Your answer, wisdom and power are waiting for you. Being at church is being in the right place at the right time.

Scriptures:

Proverbs 27:12 (The Message)
A prudent person sees trouble coming and ducks; a simpleton walks in blindly and is clobbered.

Proverbs 4:3-9 (The Message)
When I was a boy at my father's knee, the pride and joy of my mother, He would sit me down and drill me: "Take this to heart. Do what I tell you—live! Sell everything and buy Wisdom! Forage for Understanding! Don't forget one word! Don't deviate an inch!
Never walk away from Wisdom—she guards your life; love her—she keeps her eye on you. Above all and before all, do this: Get Wisdom!
Write this at the top of your list: Get Understanding! Throw your arms around her—believe me, you won't regret it; never let her go—she'll make your life glorious. She'll garland your life with grace,
she'll festoon your days with beauty."

Chapter 2

Who Do You Trust?

Psalm 20:7 (The Message)
See those people polishing their chariots, and those others grooming their horses? But we're making garlands for GOD our God. The chariots will rust, those horses pull up lame— and we'll be on our feet, standing tall.

Every morning most of us jump into our car, pop the key in the ignition, start the engine and go! We do this not knowing the mechanics of the car or how the engine works, or about all the hundreds of different components that work together to run the car. We just 'trust' it will all work fine, and most of the time it does! We literally put our lives in the hands of a bit of metal with wheels, with little or no thought.

Our life with God would be so much more fulfilling if we put that sort of 'trust' in Him and His Word. As human beings, we seem to trust more in what we can see than what we can't, but Paul encourages us to trust in God and the unseen things of this world (2 Corinthians 4: 18).

To become a person of faith requires obedience, which takes trusting God at His Word. If you trust that God has His best for you then you will never worry, you will never get anxious and you will never get discouraged. In Matthew 6:25-34, Jesus asks His disciples not to worry about food, water or clothes; just to seek God's Kingdom first. If you do that, then all the things you need will be provided. This all sounds great, but it requires that we trust God and not worry about food, water, clothes or the future. Are you a person who worries about everything? To live that way is totally against what the entire Bible teaches and what Jesus Himself stood for.

Paul tells us, in Philippians 4:6, not to get anxious about anything but to pray and offer petitions of prayer to God, and the peace of God will help you in the battle of your mind and heart. Why not decide today to be a person who will trust God *more* and worry *less*? We often find it easy to trust in temporary things like cars and aeroplanes; why not trust in God?

What Does This Mean To Me?

1. I Don't Worry!

Worry is a sin, the Bible simply says: "Do not worry!" Ask God today, through the person of the Holy Spirit, to help you identify weak areas in your life that cause you to worry. We overcome the battles in our lives by the Word of God. Jesus gave us an example in Luke 4:1-13, when He was tempted by the devil. How often do you worry? Have any of your fears come true? Learn to let go and let God take control.

2. I Don't Rely On This World

To rely on this world to provide happiness, security and hope is only going to bring discouragement, sadness and hopelessness. This world and everything it provides will not last. In John 16:33 Jesus said to his disciples, "In this world you will have trouble..." This is an important fact to note. Everything that this world has to offer will bring trouble. Jesus then goes on to say, "take heart, I have overcome the world." The greatest battle we will have is this; although we live *in* the world we must remember we are not *of* this world (John 15:18-19).

The Children of Israel left Egypt but Egypt had not really left them. Are you worldly in your thinking, your attitudes and your trust? (Romans 12:1-2)

3. I Daily Read His Word

You don't need a TV preacher, a novel or even a bestselling author's words to help you through life - God has given us His Word to help and guide us! His Word is like a lamp; it is food, comfort, safety and encouragement (Psalms 18:30; 33:4; 56:4; 107:20; 119:9 &16 & 28). His Word will help you in your darkest hour; it will bring strength to you in times of weakness and it will cause you to grow.

Scripture:

Psalm 4:5 (New Living Translation)
*Offer sacrifices in the right spirit, and trust the L*ORD.

Chapter 3
Faith & Finances

Hebrews 6:1-3 (New Living Translation)

[1]So let us stop going over the basic teachings about Christ again and again. Let us go on instead and become mature in our understanding. Surely we don't need to start again with the fundamental importance of repenting from evil deeds and placing our faith in God. [2]You don't need further instruction about baptisms, the laying on of hands, the resurrection of the dead, and eternal judgment. [3]And so, God willing, we will move forward to further understanding.

Faith should be our first response to God's Word. When He (the creator of the heavens and earth) speaks, by faith we choose to respond to His words. When God spoke to His leaders and people in the Bible, they had to respond by faith without necessarily being able to see that which God said He would do. Take the example of Noah. He had to build an ark as it was going to rain for forty days and forty nights. Now that's fine but the Bible says "it had never rained on the earth!" Noah had never seen rain, much less a boat! Joshua, by faith, had to shout the walls of Jericho down; it had never been done before. How about Moses who had to lead the people out of Egypt across the Red Sea, trusting God every step of the way?

Even the Apostle Paul had to endure hardships, trials, hunger, nakedness and shipwreck. What was it for? To build a Church that will change the history of the world. All of this was done by faith! (Hebrews 11:6)

Everything In The Kingdom Of God Operates By Faith

1. We are saved by Faith.
2. We are baptized by Faith.
3. We receive the Holy Spirit by Faith.
4. We speak in tongues by Faith.
5. We worship in Faith.
6. We pray in Faith.
7. We read the word by Faith.
8. We receive communion by Faith.
9. We are healed by Faith.
10. We minister to people in Faith.
11. We gather for meetings in Faith.
12. We tithe by Faith.
13. We give our offerings in Faith.
14. We witness by Faith.
15. We give our First Fruits by Faith.

A Great Quote:
"Faith links us with God, and is the assurance that the revealed things promised in the future are true, and that the unseen things are real! Faith is certain that what it believes is true, and that what it expects will come. It is not the hope which looks forward with wishful longing; it is the hope which looks forward with utter certainty. It is not hope which takes refuge in "perhaps"; it is the hope which is founded on a conviction. The future and the unseen can be made real for me by faith."

Practical Steps In Giving Your First And Best To God:

1. Raise your faith level daily through reading and meditating on the Word (Joshua 1:8, Psalm 1:1; Romans 10:17).

2. Pray in faith for an extended period of time every day (Matthew 6:9; 26:40; 1 Thessalonians 5:17).

3. Be faithful to church meetings and continue in worship and fellowship with other faith filled believers (Acts 2:42; Hebrews 10:25).

4. Stay in covenant relationship with God by giving what you promised (Matthew 6:33; Proverbs 3:9-10; Malachi 3:10; Luke 6:38).

5. Confess the Word of faith, by quoting scriptures in the midst of all kinds of situations (Matthew 4:4, 7, 10).

6. Cultivate Kingdom attitudes of faith in every circumstance (Romans 14:17).

7. Choose to rejoice and be happy as the Lord loves a cheerful giver! Don't tolerate discouragement or negative spirits in your life (Philippians 4:4; 2 Timothy 1:7; Hebrews 12: 3-5).

8. Exercise faith for healing in times of sickness (1 Peter 2:24; James 5:15; Matthew 15:28; Acts 14:9).

9. Take control over your thought-life (2 Corinthians 10:3-5; Ephesians 6: 10-18).

10. Live in faith by walking in total obedience to God's Word. Faithfully give God first place (Matthew 6:33; 7: 24-25).

Important Things To Do:

1. I Will Start By Giving The Little I Have

Don't wait for the full amount to come in, give what you have. Remember when Jesus fed the 5000; He used the little which was given in obedience. A little in the hands of God becomes much!

2. I Will Not Let Fear Rule My Emotions

I take captive every thought and bring it in submission to Jesus. God has not given me the spirit of fear! I will trust in Him with all my heart and lean not on my own understanding (Proverbs 3: 5-6).

3. I Will Honour God First

I choose to put Him in first place above everything else. My time, treasure, talent and touch belong to him. I seek Him and His kingdom first, knowing that He will provide all things. Choose your friends wisely. Always surround yourself with people of Faith. Starve your doubts by feeding your Faith.

Scriptures:

Matthew 6:33 (Contemporary English Version)
But more than anything else, put God's work first and do what he wants. Then the other things will be yours as well.

2 Corinthians 5:7 (Amplified Bible)
For we walk by faith [we regulate our lives and conduct ourselves by our conviction or belief respecting man's relationship to God and divine things, with trust and holy fervor; thus we walk] not by sight or appearance.

Hebrews 11:39-40 (Contemporary English Version)
[39]*All of them pleased God because of their faith! But still they died without being given what had been promised.* [40]*This was because God had something better in store for us. And he did not want them to reach the goal of their faith without us.*

Recommended Reading:

Great Faith and *Prosperity With A Purpose* by Dr. Wendell Smith

Available from www.thecitychurch.org

Chapter 4

Forgiveness

Colossians 3:13 (New International Version)
Bear with each other and forgive whatever grievances you may have against one another. Forgive as the Lord forgave you.

"If you could lick my heart, it would poison you" *(a line spoken by Claude Landsmann's "Shoah" one of the leaders of the Warsaw Uprising during World War II).*

What a powerful but sad statement! So many people today walk around with infected hearts - not caused by poor eating habits or alcohol - but by unforgiveness. Unforgiveness can lead to bitterness which can ruin a life forever. There is only one true example when it comes to forgiveness and that is Jesus. When Jesus went to the cross it was not only to provide a sacrifice for sin, but also an example for us when it comes to forgiveness. He did it so well when He said those powerful words "Father, forgive them." He was not just glossing over the evil of the heart of man, but rather highlighting the goodness and greatness of the heart of God.

Forgiveness for God was costly. It cost Him His Son; however unforgiveness for us may be even more costly, as it may cost us our very lives! Many people are in hospitals today because of unforgiveness.

The ultimate example of forgiveness is seen best in the cross of Jesus Christ. In the Cross I see the greatest price ever paid for forgiveness, but also the greatest good gained in rebuilding life! The cross of Christ does not play down evil or spin over truth; rather, it shows evil at its ugliest, while offering a new beginning in the most profound sense of the term. But the grace of forgiveness, because God Himself has paid the price for our sinful hearts, is unique to Christianity and stands superbly over and against our hate- and poison-filled, unforgiving world.

My To-Do List:

1. Forgive One Another

We are commanded to forgive one another. It is never going to be easy, but it is just simply forgiving like Christ has forgiven us. Today, ask God to search your heart through the Holy Spirit and let him show you any areas in your life where you need to repent or forgive.

2. Learn To Apologise

When you mess up, don't ever think that your title or position makes you above saying the words "I am sorry". We need to know what it means to apologise for wrongdoing. When we say we are sorry, it actually strengthens our relationships with each other and makes them even more watertight. I read once how a father punished a son for something the father thought he had done, and never listened to the child's plea, wrongly chastising the innocent. When we choose not to say sorry, we too are punishing the innocent.

3. Choose Not To Be Offended

To get offended is a choice! You can choose to be offended or choose not to get offended. People will wrong you and hurt you, but take a lesson out of the life of Joseph; you can never be the victor with a victim mentality. Joseph had the right to be bitter against his family, bosses, friends and even God. But he chose to be better than the situation and live in a higher understanding of what it means to forgive (read Genesis 37-45).

Scriptures:

Genesis 45:3-5 (New International Version)
³Joseph said to his brothers, "I am Joseph! Is my father still living?" But his brothers were not able to answer him, because they were terrified at his presence. ⁴Then Joseph said to his brothers, "Come close to me." When they had done so, he said, "I am your brother Joseph, the one you sold into Egypt! ⁵And now, do not be distressed and do not be angry with yourselves for selling me here, because it was to save lives that God sent me ahead of you.

Matthew 18:32-35 (New Living Translation)
³²Then the king called in the man he had forgiven and said, 'You evil servant! I forgave you that tremendous debt because you pleaded with me. ³³Shouldn't you have mercy on your fellow servant, just as I had mercy on you?' ³⁴Then the angry king sent the man to prison to be tortured until he had paid his entire debt. ³⁵"That's what my heavenly Father will do to you if you refuse to forgive your brothers and sisters from your heart."

Romans 4:7 (Amplified Bible)
Blessed and happy and to be envied are those whose iniquities are forgiven and whose sins are covered up and completely buried.

Chapter 5
Our Greatest Weapon Ever!

John 14:15 (New Living Translation)
"If you love me, obey my commandments."

One of the greatest weapons we have as believers is simply 'obedience.' To obey God is the greatest thing a human being can do - greater than prayer, greater than worship and greater than fasting!

Obedience leads us to do all those things regardless of whether we feel like it or not. Hebrews 11 has been labeled the 'Great Faith Chapter'. I disagree with that; I think it should be the 'Great Obedience Chapter.' Without great obedience there can never be great faith! Hebrews 11:6 says "without faith it's impossible to please God." Why? Because faith requires blind obedience to God and His Word. No options, no emotions, no feelings - just obedience. When it comes to giving our 4 T's (Time, Treasure, Talent and Touch) we are required to obey first!

Matthew 6:33 says, "But seek first His kingdom and His righteousness, and all these things will be given to you as well." Notice where our priority lies; seeking His Kingdom first. Only when we put Him first - with our income, with our lives and with obedience - will we ever live a happy, blessed and fulfilled life.

You can attend church all your life and still go to Hell for a lack of obedience. It's not just about ticking the box of salvation and then doing what we want. It's walking in obedience to Him and His Word.

Matthew 7:24 says "Therefore everyone who hears these words of mine and puts them into practice (or obeys them) is like a wise man who built his house on the rock." Why not take a moment now and ask the Holy Spirit to show you areas in your life where you need to obey God fully.

So What Does This Mean To Me?

1. I Will Daily Choose To Follow Him And His Word

We all have the freedom of choice when it comes to God and His Word. Most of the problems we face in life have nothing to do with the devil or demons, but are created by ourselves through a lack of obedience.

1 Samuel 15:22
'But Samuel replied:"Does the LORD delight in burnt offerings and sacrifices as much as in obeying the voice of the LORD? To obey is better than sacrifice, and to heed is better than the fat of rams."

2. I Will Give What's Due To Him

When we give to God, we are blessed not because of what we give, but because we choose to obey Him. When it comes to giving our tithes, offerings and first fruits, these are all locked into our obedience to God rather than merely putting money in a bucket.

3. Today's Obedience Is Tomorrows Miracle

The miracle we are waiting for, that which we really need, depends on our obedience to God first. Our miracle can be just around the corner; for our business, for our families, for our church and for our future. All that is required of us is total, 100 percent obedience to His Word.

Scriptures:

Psalm 119:17 (New International Version)
Do good to your servant, and I will live; I will obey your word.

Psalm 119:101 (Contemporary English Version)
Obey your word instead of following a way that leads to trouble.

John 14:23 (New Living Translation)
Jesus replied, "All who love me will do what I say. My Father will love them, and we will come and make our home with each of them.

Chapter 6

How Much Longer?

Psalm 27:14 (Amplified Bible)
Wait and hope for and expect the Lord; be brave and of good courage and let your heart be stout and enduring. Yes, wait for and hope for and expect the Lord.

I don't enjoy waiting; in fact I really dislike it. I often travel to various parts of the world to speak in churches and at conferences and the worst part for me is waiting! Waiting in airports, waiting for lifts - even waiting in life for God to do what He said He will do. I find it all frustrating. However, we must remember that our waiting for the things of God is not in vain.

He will come through. For every instance of bad news there will be good news, for every disappointment an opportunity will open up and in every seemingly upturned situation, God is working out something far better than we can see.

Romans 8:28 tells us that "all things work together for the good of those who love Him."

Sometimes I don't understand this scripture in the light of human suffering and unfulfilled promises, but I still put my trust in Him that good can come out of a bad situation.

We often try to work out everything with human wisdom and human understanding. We must remember that 'His ways are not our ways', we need to 'focus on the unseen', we need to 'lean not on our own understanding', but in everything we do wait on the Lord. Those who do will 'renew their strength, mount up with wings as eagles, run and not grow weary, walk and shall not faint' (Isaiah 55:7-11; 2 Corinthians 4:18; Proverbs 3:5; Isaiah 40:31).

Life is not always fair, not always just and not always right, but the one thing we should do is keep our eyes on Him. If we do that then the problems and trials of this world will grow dim. Paul puts it this way in Philippians 3:13-14, "one thing I do: forgetting what is behind and straining toward what is ahead, I press on..."

Discouragement can come creeping in when we are in the midst of life's darkest moments; however, take a minute, lift your eyes above the mountains, see beyond the disappointment, and watch how He will deliver you from your very hour of darkness.

He will never leave you nor forsake you. Your waiting is not in vain!

What Does This Mean To Me?

1. God Has My Best Interests In Mind

In times of waiting it can seem that 'I am not important to God'. Well, you are important to God! He loves you and has your best interests at heart. He knows what you need; He will provide a way and give you the ability to overcome what seems to be an impossible situation. He is God and He reigns.

(Please read and pray through Matthew 6: 25-33; Psalm 91 and Psalm 27)

2. I Will Gather For Church With My Brothers And Sisters

There is strength in church, when we gather with our spiritual family. We should not miss church or stay home during the storms of life. Rather, we should assemble together, build on the rock of His Word and when the storms of life come we will be able to stand. The church will provide shelter, help and encouragement during these low times and especially when we are in a season of waiting (Hebrews 10:25; Matthew 7: 24-27).

3. Don't Give Up!

It's easy to get discouraged during these seasons of waiting and what seems like un-answered prayer. The temptation to give up will be stronger than ever during these times. Remember; never give up on God, He has not given up on you!

Don't stop responding and praying for healing; don't stop believing and don't stop having faith. Now, even more than ever, press on, strain forward. God has not forgotten you; God has not left you behind. Your answer will come; your moment for healing will come. Don't give up! Your answer is right around the corner.

Scripture:

Psalm 121:1-2 (New Living Translation)
[1]*I look up to the mountains—does my help come from there?*
[2]*My help comes from the Lord, who made heaven and earth!*

Chapter 7

Tough Times & God

Genesis 26:12-14 (The Message)
*Isaac planted crops in that land and took in a huge harvest. GOD blessed him.
The man got richer and richer by the day until he was very wealthy. He
accumulated flocks and herds and many, many servants, so much so that the
Philistines began to envy him..."*

Blessings and riches can be great and awesome as God opens the windows of
heaven and blesses His people for obedience in bringing the tithe and first fruits
offering (Malachi 3:10-12). Isaac did exactly that - despite the gloomy forecast
about the land in which he lived (it was double famine), he still planted in that
land as God commanded him to do and reaped the rewards of obedience to
God.

God blesses us when we obey Him above anyone and anything else. Obedience
is when we do what God asks of us despite what we see around us. In 2
Corinthians 4:16-18, Paul asks the believers to fix their eyes on the unseen and
the eternal and when we do that we are daily renewed.

Isaac would have seen the effects of 'the credit crunch', but he chose to do
what God asked him to do and not what everyone else was doing.

Romans 8:15 says "For you did not receive a spirit that makes you a slave again
to fear, but you received the Spirit of sonship. And by him we cry, "Abba,
Father."" We are not to be fearful in these times, but full of faith. In fact we

should be faith~full; faithful to God as He will never let you down. Why not take a moment now and read through Psalm 91 and list out some God thoughts and Holy Spirit promptings.

Things to Remember:

1. Be Faithful In Giving Your Tithes And Offerings

Giving to God is all about total obedience and not about how you feel or whether you can afford to or not. No matter what you go through in life, God promises never to leave us or forsake us. He is totally committed to your well-being.

Are you totally committed to Him by bringing your tithes and offerings (including your First Fruits)? Bring your offerings this Sunday and watch a huge harvest come your way!

2. Be In Church

I firmly believe that there's no better place to be than church. Whenever the church doors open we should be there! David was exceedingly happy when it was time for church (Psalm 122:1). Why? Because he knew God was going to be there and that in His presence there is joy and blessing. In Hebrews 10:25, Paul admonishes believers not to miss church, as you may just be missing your moment of breakthrough.

3. The Worst Is Behind You

Your future is brighter than your past. Your financial breakthrough is just around the corner - it's actually closer than you think. The only thing that stops blessings is disobedience.

The level of your obedience determines your level of blessing. Just remember that today's obedience is tomorrow's miracle. As leaders, partners and people of faith we press on, we give, we fight the good fight.

How? By planting seeds in His kingdom. By storing up treasure where moth, rust and thieves cannot break in. When we do this, we will all reap a huge harvest.

Scriptures:

Galatians 6:7 (New Living Translation)
Don't be misled—you cannot mock the justice of God. You will always harvest what you plant.

Luke 6:38 (Amplified Bible)
Give, and [gifts] will be given to you; good measure, pressed down, shaken together, and running over, will they pour into [the pouch formed by] the bosom [of your robe and used as a bag]. For with the measure you deal out [with the measure you use when you confer benefits on others], it will be measured back to you.

Chapter 8

Big Fish, Big Provision!

Matthew 17:27 (New Living Translation)
However, we don't want to offend them, so go down to the lake and throw in a line. Open the mouth of the first fish you catch, and you will find a large silver coin. Take it and pay the tax for both of us."

I have so many memories of fishing with my father and two brothers in Trinidad. One particular occasion that comes to mind is on Saturday when we were all very excited about going fishing. One of the important things in sea-shore fishing is having the right bait; however this particular weekend was carnival weekend in Trinidad, so most businesses and shops were closed. Try as we might we could not find any bait! As a young child I said to my father, "You are a preacher and you know God, why don't you ask Him to give us some bait?" This was said more out of frustration than faith, however my father replied, "Do you believe that He can give us bait?!" "Yes", I answered. Then he said "So let's pray now and ask Him to supply some bait." With my two brothers laughing at me, I had to pray out loud in the car park and ask God Almighty for bait!

We packed the car and headed to the beach. Upon arriving at the beach the tide was low, so low that all the rocks were exposed with little pools around them. As I ran down to the pools, to my surprise they were stuffed full of prawns. So many prawns, in fact, that we collected a few buckets full which provided excellent bait and were good for eating as well! That day we caught so many fish that it was, for me, a supernatural miracle of Gods provision.

Although that was just a small miracle in my life, I will never forget it. It's that same belief in God that has caused my wife and I to buy our house, our car and our first church building. It's that same child-like faith that caused my eyes to see healing and miracles in our lives and the lives of other people.

God will provide for all our needs, but we've got our part to do. You cannot just do nothing and expect God's blessing or provision. Peter had to go to the lake and throw a line, then catch the fish and open its mouth. God will provide, but you've always got to do what He asks of you first. It can never be 'on your terms', but always on His command. Without faith it is impossible to please God (Hebrews 11:6). Today, take that step of faith with your finances and put Him first! Give and you will be blessed (Luke 6:38).

By the way, some of you may be thinking, "How do you know it was a big fish?" Well, a small fish cannot hold a large coin in its mouth!

So What Do I Do?

1.   Obey First!

When it comes to seeing great provision, it will require great obedience. There's only one thing God blesses His people for and that's obedience. To obey God is better than sacrifice (I Samuel 15:22). When it comes to obedience, what matters most is what He says and not what we feel about the situation.

2.   Put God First.

God wants first place in our lives, not only on Sunday but every day of the week. Without Him having first place we will not have the first and best in our lives. So many people want God's best but fail to put Him and His house first. Putting God first starts in the heart and works its way out in how we live and what we do with our lives (Deuteronomy 26; Matthew 6:33).

3. Trust Him.

One of my favourite verses in the Bible, when it comes to how we live our lives, is found in Proverbs 3:5-6. It simply asks us to trust God and not even try and think about it. In everything we do acknowledge Him as Lord and He will make our paths straight. Trust is simply "letting go and letting God." Let go of your future, your hopes and your dreams, and give it all to God. Then watch how God will provide all your needs, as His river of supply never runs dry.

Scriptures:

Proverbs 3:5-6 (Contemporary English Version)
*[5]With all your heart you must trust the LORD and not your own judgment.
[6]Always let him lead you, and he will clear the road for you to follow.*

Matthew 6:33 (Contemporary English Version)
But more than anything else, put God's work first and do what he wants. Then the other things will be yours as well.

Section 2

Church

Chapter 9

What Makes You Happy?

Hebrews 13:5 (New Living Translation)
*Don't love money; be satisfied with what you have. For God has said, "I will
never fail you. I will never abandon you."*

Deuteronomy 31:6 (The Message)
*"Be strong. Take courage. Don't be intimidated. Don't give them a second
thought because God, your God, is striding ahead of you. He's right there with
you. He won't let you down; he won't leave you."*

As the old *Rolling Stones* song goes "I can't get no...satisfaction". Along with
Mick Jagger and others, we live in a world today where most people – even
believers – can become dissatisfied with life, with what they have and what
they do. Money can also bring dissatisfaction. We can never seem to have
enough. No matter what you buy, it seems to be only a little while until a new
model or upgraded version comes out and you, like me, hear "Dad, that's so
outdated!"

The writer of Hebrews encourages his readers to be happy with what they have!
This does not mean we shouldn't believe for God's blessings and abundance in
our lives; we should not walk around with a mentality that says 'this is my lot in
life.' In order to get what we need out of life, we should seek God's kingdom
first. Matthew 6:23-33 gives us a great revelation about how God's blessings
work. We should not seek the things we need, as pagans or worldly people do,

but we should put God first! We are to put God first with our time, with our treasure, with our talent and with our one-to-one touch.

Remember God is our source; He is our helper and the one that provides for our every need. He knows what you need and when you need it. Fear will often come knocking on the door of our lives when we cannot make ends meet, pay the bills or help the needy. But let God be God and trust Him today. Be happy with what you've got and put God first! If you do, then the blessings of God will come your way. Here's a wise saying of my father Dr. Tony Kawalsingh, "The devil has nothing to offer a rejoicing Believer."

What Does This Mean To Me?

1. Stronger Church Equals A Changed Society

As the Church gets stronger, so its influence and ability to reach out will increase. It takes money to build Church, reach the lost and help the needy. There seem to be two camps in Christianity when it comes to money. Firstly, there are those that say we should sell all that we have and help the poor and needy, not 'wasting' money on church buildings but spending it on the more urgent needs of the poor. Also, there are those who say that the more money we have, the greater our faith must be. These two positions are equally wrong. The problem is not money, but how we view it. We need money to purchase church buildings, look after the harvest of souls and help the needy, but having money is not a sign of great faith; just good business practice, hard work and Gods provision! Our focus should never be money, but God. Remember that the Church, not human reasoning, is God's plan to bring change on the earth (Matthew 16:13-19).

2. Give First To God And Build His Church

In John 12:1-8, we read of Mary taking expensive perfume and pouring it on the feet of Jesus. Judas objected; 'This could have been sold and given to the poor!' It was worth the equivalent of 1 year's wages. However, the verse says, 'not that he cared for the poor'. Judas had a problem with money and used the poor as an excuse to justify his sin, which was stealing from the money bag. You may not be stealing from the church offering bucket, but according to Malachi 3:8-12, if you are withholding your tithes and offerings, you are doing just that!

3.   Jesus And His Bride The Church Deserve The Best!

Jesus commended the woman for what she did as it was for Him. In John 12:8 Jesus said, "You will always have the poor, but you will not always have me!" If anyone could have stopped poverty it was Jesus. But He did not. Human reasoning is not the solution to worldwide problems; Jesus and His Church are. Remember that Jesus was not poor, but equally He didn't depend on money for His source. When it comes to giving to God, the Church is His designated conduit; not TV ministries, or other well meaning Para-church organisations but the local church.

The church represents Christ; as we reflect Him to our society it should be a reflection of comfort, excellence and the best of what is available today. When the tabernacle of Moses, David and Solomon was built, it was done so using only the best materials available. The purest silver and gold, the finest materials and only the best imported cedars would do. Why? It represents our God! He surely deserves our best! Money will not bring you total satisfaction, but Jesus will as He brings joy and fulfilment to your life.

Scriptures:

1 Chronicles 15:16 (New International Version)
David told the leaders of the Levites to appoint their brothers as singers to sing joyful songs, accompanied by musical instruments: lyres, harps and cymbals.

Psalm 21:6 (Amplified Bible)
For You make him to be blessed and a blessing forever; You make him exceedingly glad with the joy of Your presence.

Proverbs 3:5 (New International Version)
"Trust in the Lord with all of your heart and lean not on your own understanding; in all your ways submit to Him and He will make your paths straight."

Chapter 10

No Problem, Man!

John 15:7 (New Living Translation)
But if you remain in me and my words remain in you, you may ask for anything you want, and it will be granted!

One of the things about growing up in Trinidad and Tobago is that no one is ever in a hurry to do anything. It's what West Indians call the rhythm of the Caribbean. "No problem Man! Don't worry, don't fret Man!"

Having not lived in Trinidad for some 16 years now, whenever I visit the place it can be quite frustrating as I am now used to a different pace of life. I must now re-adjust and slow right down to the rhythm of the Caribbean.

We live in a world today where everyone is on the go! We can be all over the place, even travelling all over the world, every week. Life seems to be getting faster and faster. Kids are growing up rapidly and families are losing connection with each other whilst living under the same roof!

However, when it comes to our walk with Jesus we need to slow the pace right down. Adopt the West Indian mentality and relax and wait on God.

Remaining in God is the best placement you could ever have. It's only then that we can truly be fruitful and be truly blessed. Our prayer life becomes even more fruitful if we remain in Him, when we don't worry and fret...Man!

When it comes to courting or finding a future wife or husband, the first step for both people involved is to be connected to Him and to remain in Him. Then let God through time, character and the guidance of your pastors, lift you to the next level. Only then will relationships last.

Not only are we to remain in Him but also His words must remain in us. It's not just waiting empty minded, but with the Word of the Lord to hand and mind. Read your Bible, pray, fast and seek God. Waited time is not wasted time if we are in Christ. As we wait on God we get strength, power and grace to do all that God has called us to do, and even more importantly, we go on to bear much fruit!

Isaiah 40:28-31 (Amplified Bible)
Have you not known? Have you not heard? The everlasting God, the Lord, the Creator of the ends of the earth, does not faint or grow weary; there is no searching of His understanding. **He gives power to the faint and weary, and to him who has no might He increases strength** *[causing it to multiply and making it to abound]. Even youths shall faint and be weary, and [selected] young men shall feebly stumble and fall exhausted;* **But those who wait for the Lord [who expect, look for, and hope in Him] shall change and renew their strength and power; they shall lift their wings and mount up [close to God] as eagles [mount up to the sun]; they shall run and not be weary, they shall walk and not faint or become tired.**

So in the midst of a worldwide economic crisis, the best thing you can do is wait on God and let His words remain in you. Just watch - as you stay put, blessing will come your way!

My To-Do List!

1. I Wait On God In Church

Whilst waiting, it is important to be in the right place at the right time. You can wait in the wrong place and miss your appointed time. The New Testament scriptures are written mostly to local churches, and that is where we are called to be. To love God means you love church. You cannot separate one from the other. The church is the body, the bride of Christ and it belongs to Jesus. Make sure you're in church 100% and always on time!

Psalm 27:4; Matthew 16:17-19; Ephesians 2:19-20; 3: 10; Hebrews 10:25.

2. Develop A Personal Devotion

This is a time set aside every day to sit and read the Bible and make special note of any God thoughts or Holy Spirit promptings. These times help us to grow and bear much fruit. They also help us to get the Word of the Lord deep within, hidden in our hearts. Teach your children to pray, to read their Bibles every day, and let them see you doing it.

As you develop this, a hunger and passion for the things of God will be re-fuelled, and also the promise of blessing awaits you!

Genesis 19:27; Psalm 119: 10-11 & 145-147; Matthew 6:25-33.

Scriptures:

Ephesians 2:19-20 (Amplified Bible)
[19]Therefore you are no longer outsiders (exiles, migrants, and aliens, excluded from the rights of citizens), but you now share citizenship with the saints (God's own people, consecrated and set apart for Himself); and you belong to God's [own] household. [20]You are built upon the foundation of the apostles and prophets with Christ Jesus Himself the chief Cornerstone.

Psalm 119:10-11 (New International Version)
[10]I seek you with all my heart;
   do not let me stray from your commands.
[11]I have hidden your word in my heart
   that I might not sin against you.

Chapter 11

Wise Or Foolish?

Proverbs 12:15 (New Living Translation)
Fools think their own way is right, but the wise listen to others.

Life is full of choices, we all make them daily. Some choices require no need to ask for advice; they are what the Americans call 'no brainers.' Other choices, however, require time, prayer, God's Word and godly council.

The book of Proverbs was written for Solomon's son Rehoboam, whom you can read about in 1 Kings 12. Proverbs was written as a collection of wise sayings and proverbs to help Rehoboam run a kingdom. Rehoboam had a decision to make (1 Kings 12: 6) and he did the right thing by consulting the elders, who had also counselled his father Solomon. However he also asked advice from some friends he grew up with. The upshot was that he listened to his friends over the elders and the result was not good! Take some time and read verses 8-10.

The Bible has given us pastors and elders in the church to help give advice and godly council (Ephesians 4:11-12; Hebrews 13:17). However many people, upon hearing what they say, choose to ignore it and listen to friends and family instead. This often leads to hardship, broken hearts and a ruined life (Proverbs 15:22).

The TV show American Idol makes for some hilarious viewing. You will often see contestants who really cannot sing at all, and not only is this clear to the judges but also to we the viewers! But some of the contestants, no matter how clearly the judges tell them they cannot sing, will not listen to them. Why? "Because my Mum, Dad, Grandma, Grandpa and friends say I am an excellent singer." These people are not qualified to give advice on singing and record contracts, but people like to listen to them instead of those who are qualified in this field. So it is with life, many people are not qualified to give advice about life but they will happily give it to you. However you should not listen to them. God has set up His Church, His bride, where you can be helped and equipped with the answers that are needed for successful living.

I often hear people say, 'all you need is a good attitude in life and you will succeed.' To a certain extent that is right, however you could have a good attitude as you travel on the wrong road and it will not change the fact that you are heading in the wrong direction until it's too late! Attitude is not everything.

Seek godly advice and wisdom to make right choices (Proverbs 116:3; 9:21; 20:18).

Questions To Answer:

1. Do You Belong To A Church?

Church is not a place you should just attend, you should belong there. Your roots should go down deep and you should become a devoted committed member. Who speaks into your life? Are you on par with those around you? This has nothing to do with age but rather with calling. You will never have a 'happy ever after' if you are not accountable to anyone. Never listen to those who are not accountable to anyone. Even the Disciples of Christ reported back things they had seen and heard, showing the principle of accountability at work (1 John 1:3; Mark 6:30; Luke 9:10; Acts 4:23; 15:4; 1 Corinthians 5:1).

2. Do You Filter Every Decision Through The Word?

To make decisions based on how you feel is to let your emotions rule your judgment. Pilots, when doing their training, are taught to ignore feelings and keep their eyes on the instrument panel. Why? Because you can often feel things that simply are not true. Feelings are like water; no matter what you pour them into, they will take on that shape. You can convince yourself that a way is right until you check it out on a map. You need a reliable guide. Trust in God and His words and don't let your emotions rule your decision making (Proverbs 3:5; 30:5; Psalm 12:6; 119:101).

Scriptures:

1 Timothy 3:15 (Amplified Bible)
If I am detained, you may know how people ought to conduct themselves in the household of God, which is the church of the living God, the pillar and stay (the prop and support) of the Truth.

Ephesians 1:21-23 (New International Version)
[21]Far above all rule and authority, power and dominion, and every title that can be given, not only in the present age but also in the one to come. [22]And **God placed all things under his feet and appointed him to be head over everything for the church,** *[23]which is his body, the fullness of him who fills everything in every way.*

Ephesians 3:10 (New International Version)
*His intent was that now, **through the church**, the manifold wisdom of God should be made known to the rulers and authorities in the heavenly realms.*

Chapter 12

What Comes Out of Your Mouth?

1 Timothy 6:20-21 (New Living Translation)
[20]Timothy, guard what God has entrusted to you. Avoid godless, foolish discussions with those who oppose you with their so-called knowledge. [21]Some people have wandered from the faith by following such foolishness. May God's grace be with you all.

Sports can be exciting, exhilarating and total fun! In most sports across the world there are people who are called 'armchair professionals'. These people can tell who isn't pulling their weight, why the coaches need to be changed and what the 'useless' team needs to do to win. These so called 'experts' have the answer to bring victory at every game, every time! The fact of the matter is that the guys on the field are trained to play the game and the coaches are qualified and chosen to lead and manage the team. The coaching staff has put in countless hours of work on game plans, strategies and practises that put them ahead in their chosen profession. They are doing the job and playing the games to the best of their ability and all they need is support and encouragement from the fans, even if they lose a game!

In the church world we can get 'church professionals' who think they know better. They claim to know the Bible better than most, and are ready to share their professional concerns - to anyone who will listen to them - as to what the church should be doing and how the church should function. These people, if entertained, can cause you to lose your joy and even to walk away from the faith. Paul calls this 'foolish chatter', and 'so-called knowledge'. He commands Timothy to guard himself against such chatter and not to follow such foolishness.

Acts gives a great picture of what church should be like. Take a moment and read this scripture:

Acts 2:42-47 (New International Version)
[42]They devoted themselves to the apostles' teaching and to fellowship, to the breaking of bread and to prayer. [43]Everyone was filled with awe, and many wonders and miraculous signs were done by the apostles. [44]All the believers were together and had everything in common. [45]Selling their possessions and goods, they gave to anyone as he had need. [46]Every day they continued to meet together in the temple courts. They broke bread in their homes and ate together with glad and sincere hearts, [47]praising God and enjoying the favour of all the people. And the Lord added to their number daily those who were being saved.

Notice that the opening line of this verse begins with: "They devoted themselves to the apostles' teaching and to fellowship". The early Church had just one source of the Word – the apostles' teaching (the equivalent today is the pastor of the local church), and working with a spirit of unity they built the Church and served each other. The result was fantastic! The Church grew and many new lives were touched by God. This all happened because they chose to follow one voice and moved in one direction, serving under one leadership. There are many people with opinions around today, many who 'know better' or have a 'professional opinion' as to how things should be done, but this not only ruins themselves but also those who listen to them. Be on your guard for people like this; avoid 'godless chatter' and 'foolish discussion' from those who think that they know better.

So What Does This Mean To Me?

1. Don't Entertain Negative Talk About The Church Or Its Leadership

When someone is talking negatively about Church or the leadership, they are attacking Christ and not just the leadership of the Church (see Acts 9). In Numbers 12, Miriam and Aaron opposed Moses and the Lord listened to their conversation. In verse 9, the Bible states 'The anger of the Lord burned against them...' Why? They crossed God's anointed, His choice, and to do this is to cross God himself. So what do you do if there is a genuine problem within the church? Pray and ask God to show you if it's a real problem or just an offence you have taken against a leader or something done in the Church. If so, deal with it quickly and ask your leader(s) for forgiveness.

2. Fill Your Heart With Only The Best Words

Our words can build or destroy. Life and death are in the power of the tongue. If you're going to say anything, double-check your words carefully. This is what Paul has to say about it...

Scripture:

Philippians 4:8 (The Message)
"Summing it all up, friends, I'd say you'll do best by filling your minds and meditating on things true, noble, reputable, authentic, compelling, gracious— the best, not the worst; the beautiful, not the ugly; things to praise, not things to curse. Put into practice what you learned from me, what you heard and saw and realized. Do that, and God, who makes everything work together, will work you into his most excellent harmonies."

Chapter 13
Don't Worry, Just Seek His Kingdom First!

Matthew 6:33 (Contemporary English Version)
But more than anything else, put God's work first and do what he wants. Then the other things will be yours as well.

Why do we worry, when the Lord himself tells us not to worry?! Worry can be a disease that is very infectious in our society. We need to see worry for what it really is, and to avoid the evil temptation to worry. Here are seven things to consider about worry:

1. Worry is a sin
2. Worry is a thief
3. Worry magnifies lies
4. Worry will distort fact and truth
5. Worry will stop you hearing from God
6. Worry kills your potential
7. Worry, if you let it, can be a life-master

When we worry, we are not seeking His Kingdom first; we are actually trying to work things out by ourselves and not letting Him take care of all our needs.

Chip Kawalsingh

Don't worry! Leaving the issue of worry behind for a moment, let's look at seeking His Kingdom first.

We live in a culture today where people like to identify with their own. We see certain races of people wanting to stick with their own tribe or what they term as 'their people'. When we talk about 'our culture', we are not putting His Kingdom first; we are putting where we come from above His Kingdom. Remember, where we come from is not as important as where we are going!

To be a believer is not only to love Jesus, but to act like Him; to see the best in our brother or sister in the Lord. Romans 14:17 tells us that 'The Kingdom of God is about righteousness, peace and joy', not about 'eating or drinking'. In other words, to seek His Kingdom is not to be caught up with the daily routine of life (the 'eating and drinking') or the culture of where we come from, but to seek righteousness, peace and joy in everything.

What Does All This Mean?

1. Don't Worry

Stop worrying about life and start trusting God. To trust God is simply to let go and let Him take control. He cannot fix that which is not in His hands! (Psalm 9:10; 18:2)

2. Seek His Kingdom First

I will put God's work first, above what I want, even above my own needs and desires. To deny ourselves really means to die to 'Me'. To seek His Kingdom is to seek godly council in life choices rather than just listening to those who say what you want to hear (I Kings 12: 1-17; Hebrews 13:17).

3. See The Best In My Sister And Brother

I always see the best in others, even though they may do or say something that in our culture may be offensive. We seek His Kingdom first above our own feelings. We die to ourselves and become alive in Christ. That is, 'my identity is not in the culture of where I come from but the culture of where I am going'. I choose not to get offended, but to see the best in others.

Scriptures:

Philippians 2:5-8 (New International Version)
5Your attitude should be the same as that of Christ Jesus: 6Who, being in very nature God, did not consider equality with God something to be grasped, 7but made himself nothing, taking the very nature of a servant, being made in human likeness.8And being found in appearance as a man, he humbled himself and became obedient to death— even death on a cross!

Ephesians 4:22-24 (Contemporary English Version)
22You were told that your foolish desires will destroy you and that you must give up your old way of life with all its bad habits. 23Let the Spirit change your way of thinking 24and make you into a new person. You were created to be like God, and so you must please him and be truly holy.

Chapter 14

More Fruit

John 15:5 (New Living Translation)
"Yes, I am the vine; you are the branches. Those who remain in me, and I in them, will produce much fruit. For apart from me you can do nothing."

When we talk about serving God, it's not only what we actually do, but who we are that counts. We are called 'branches' which belong to the vine (Jesus). Our source, our strength, our identity and everything we do should be locked into the vine. If it is, then we will bear fruit. Not just any fruit, but fruit that will remain! If we do not remain in Him, Jesus says 'you can do nothing'. In other words, anything you try and do without Him will never bring fulfilment, joy and satisfaction.

In verse 2 of this chapter, Jesus says "He (the Father) cuts off every branch in **me** that bears not fruit, while every branch that bears fruit He **prunes**." Notice the two words in bold, 'me' and 'prunes'.

Firstly, the branches that bear no fruit are not the unbeliever or the unsaved, but some of those who are in Him. It is possible to be in Christ and be cut off for a lack of fruit! It's not just enough to be saved; He is after fruit in our lives. What sort of fruit are you producing in your daily walk with God?

Secondly, the branches that do bear fruit, He prunes. The word prune here does not mean the same thing as you may think. It is not a cutting off or trimming back. The word actually means 'washes'. He washes every branch that bears fruit. One of the symbols of the Holy Spirit in the Bible is water, so you may say that every branch that bears fruit, He washes by the Holy Spirit so it may produce even more. The context of John 15 has not only to do with the Father (who is the gardener), the Son (who is the vine) but also the Holy Spirit (who is our advocate). Without the Holy Spirit's help in our lives we are limited in how much fruit we can produce. You see, it's all about fruit!

Things To Action:

1. Fruitfulness Is Our Purpose

We are created to bear fruit. This is not an instant thing, but a process. What helps us to bear fruit that remains is being connected (or remaining) in Him, through His chosen instrument which is the Church. It's not enough just to be a 'Sunday Only Christian.' Going to church one day a week will only help your Christian walk so far. Think about how many hours there are in the week, and how many of those hours you spend in church! The Church is His bride, His instrument of change. Acts 9 tells us that when Saul (who became the Apostle Paul) was persecuting the Church, he was persecuting Jesus! How we treat the Church is how we treat Him! How much are you willing to give to Him? The greatest disaster in life is not death, but living life with no purpose.

2. Remaining In Him Is Our Choice

The choice of remaining is not His but ours! John 15:7 says, "If **you** remain **in me** and my words remain in you, ask whatever you wish and it will be done for you."

If we choose to stay in Him, remain and wait patiently in the vine through the instrument of the local church, then not only will we bear fruit, but also whatever we pray for will be done. The gardener (who is the Father) will cut off those branches that do not produce fruit. You see, it's all about the fruit in our lives that only comes by remaining in Him, through the local church.

Scriptures:

Galatians 5:22-23 (New Living Translation)
^{22}But the Holy Spirit produces this kind of fruit in our lives: love, joy, peace, patience, kindness, goodness, faithfulness, ^{23}gentleness, and self-control. There is no law against these things!

Colossians 1:5-7 (New Living Translation)
^{5}which come from your confident hope of what God has reserved for you in heaven. You have had this expectation ever since you first heard the truth of the Good News. ^{6}This same Good News that came to you is going out all over the world. It is bearing fruit everywhere by changing lives, just as it changed your lives from the day you first heard and understood the truth about God's wonderful grace. ^{7}You learned about the Good News from Epaphras, our beloved co-worker. He is Christ's faithful servant, and he is helping us on your behalf.

Chapter 15

Patience, My Child

Romans 8:24-25 (New International Version)
[24]*For in this hope we were saved. But hope that is seen is no hope at all. Who hopes for what he already has? [25]But if we hope for what we do not yet have, we wait for it patiently.*

Although waiting seems to have gone out of fashion today, especially with technology supposedly making our life easier, we still often end up having to wait. Waiting has never been a personal strong point for me, however the Lord seems to be teaching me more and more what it means to wait. When we wait on the Lord we put our hope in Him. We are not 'hoping' in a human-being with weaknesses and flaws, but in our Lord and King.

One of the fathers of modern fishing (and the author of the greatest angling book ever, *The Complete Angler*), Izaak Walton, wrote these profound words; "Study to be quiet." I will add to that by saying "Study to be patient." As you read this piece of well-written old English literature you soon realise that this man, Izaak Walton, was more than a fishermen - he was also a Minister of the Gospel. As I read this chapter from his book, it occurred to me that waiting patiently on the Lord is an art and grace which only comes by having hope! Yes, because of who He is and what He has done, we can wait; quietly and patiently.

As life gets busier and kids seem to grow up faster, we can get worried about many things. We must learn to 'study to be quiet," and also, "study to be patient."

Psalm 37:7 (New Living Translation)
Be still in the presence of the LORD, and wait patiently for him to act. Don't worry about evil people who prosper or fret about their wicked schemes.

Wait on the Lord; it's only in Him that you will find strength, hope and your answer.

So What Do I Do?

1. Waiting Is Not Unusual; It's Part Of The Answer!

God teaches us many lessons while we wait. Some lessons like faith, trust and hope are built and strengthened during a season of waiting. The Bible says that all the promises of the Lord are "yes" and "amen"; the Bible never said they were instant! What you do while you wait will often determine how long you wait for an answer! (2 Corinthians 1:20; 4:18)

2. Patience Is One Of The Fruits!

Part of the evidence of the Holy Spirit in our lives is seen by the fruit we produce. One of those fruits is patience. It may not be a very popular fruit, but like all fruit it is very good for you. While we wait patiently, the fruit has to go through the stages of development and then ripen, which all takes time. No farmer reaps a crop the same day he plants the seed, he must wait! When we wait we learn what true staying power is (Galatians 5:22; Ephesians 5:15-17).

3. Impatience Produces Fruit As Well!

When we act outside of waiting on God it produces fruit, but not the kind we can be proud of. Abraham and Sarah were meant to wait for God to do what He said He would do. God promised to give them a child of their own, but they couldn't wait on God patiently, so they made a plan with their maid and they produced an alternative son, Ishmael. Ishmaels are still being born today to those who cannot wait on God. The devil will often show you an alternative while you wait, however, you must resist. Stay in the Lord, wait patiently and be in church! That way the devil never gets the victory. As you wait, let these words be burnt on your heart today; "Lord I'll wait on you!" (Genesis 16; 1 Samuel 13: 7-14; Psalms 77:1-20)

Scriptures:

2 Corinthians 4:18 (New International Version)
So we fix our eyes not on what is seen, but on what is unseen. For what is seen is temporary, but what is unseen is eternal.

Galatians 5:22 (New King James Version)
But the fruit of the Spirit is love, joy, peace, longsuffering, kindness, goodness, faithfulness.

Chapter 16

Bring It On!

1 Timothy 6:12 (New Living Translation)
Fight the good fight for the true faith. Hold tightly to the eternal life to which God has called you, which you have confessed so well before many witnesses.

When we were young boys growing up in Trinidad, my brothers and I would love to listen to my dad's stories of when he was a teenager. He told one story about a time when some of the boys from his village wanted to fight him and his brothers. One day, the two groups met on the village road at dusk, toe to toe! My father pushed his way ahead of his brothers and began to shout at the other boys, knowing that his brothers were with him. Then the biggest of the boys from the other group came forward, and my dad said "Come on!", only to look over his shoulder and see his brothers running at the speed of lightning in the other direction!

Youthful scrimmages are not what Paul is talking to Timothy about, but a greater fight that we face every day. Paul would have been a real tough guy. Let's take a minute to look at some of the things he was involved in; shipwrecks, snakebites, beatings, floggings, starvation and constant, dangerous travel. He would have walked miles to get to the churches and the other places he went to. He had to be a tough guy!

Christians are meant to be a tough bunch of people. We are not meant to be spiritual wimps or those who run after the weak and ineffective things, but those who fight to the end.

What makes our spiritual muscles strong is faith! Faith is for tough times and difficult and impossible situations. You cannot fight effectively if you are unfit and untrained. You may last a round, only to be knocked down in the second. We must daily exercise our spiritual muscles in order to become great fighters for His Kingdom.

My 'To Do' List:

1. You Are In A Battle

There's a real war waging in our lives. It's not necessarily fighting the devil and his demons, but our own selfish, carnal desires (James 4: 1-4). The weapons we need are not guns and knives but spiritual amour. Ephesians 6:16 asks us to "take up the shield of faith." Daily pick up the shield of faith!

2. Church Is Your Boot Camp

Hebrews 10:25 says "Let us not give up meeting together as some are in the habit of doing, but encourage one another." Church is where we strengthen our faith, where we grow and where the army unites and becomes stronger. Church is where we treat the wounded, the hurt and dying; it's where you get nursed back to health. When you miss church you are endangering your life. I Peter 5:8 tells us that the devil prowls around like a lion; he is looking for those who are outside the flock.

3. Get The Word In You

Throughout the Bible you read, "The Word of the Lord..." There is something important about having the Word of the Lord in you. Romans 10:17 (TNIV) says, "Consequently, faith comes by hearing the message, and the message is heard through the Word". It's important to read your Bible every day, pray every day, and get the preached Word into you. Weak believers are those who miss church for trivial reasons. The hidden Word keeps us from sin and from drifting! (See Psalms 119: 11; Hebrews 2 1:-2)

Scriptures:

Psalm 35:1 (New International Version)
Contend, O LORD, with those who contend with me; fight against those who fight against me.

Matthew 11:12 (Amplified Bible)
And from the days of John the Baptist until the present time, the kingdom of heaven has endured violent assault, and violent men seize it by force [as a precious prize - a share in the heavenly kingdom is sought with most ardent zeal and intense exertion].

Philippians 3:7-9 (The Message)
The very credentials these people are waving around as something special, I'm tearing up and throwing out with the trash—along with everything else I used to take credit for. And why? Because of Christ. Yes, all the things I once thought were so important are gone from my life. Compared to the high privilege of knowing Christ Jesus as my Master, firsthand, everything I once thought I had going for me is insignificant—dog dung. I've dumped it all in the trash so that I could embrace Christ and be embraced by him. I didn't want some petty, inferior brand of righteousness that comes from keeping a list of rules when I could get the robust kind that comes from trusting Christ—God's righteousness.

Chapter 17

What Do You Live For?

Psalm 39:4-5 (Contemporary English Version)
"Please, LORD, show me my future. Will I soon be gone? You made my life short, so brief that the time means nothing to you. "Human life is but a breath."

A recent survey said that the average person in the United Kingdom watches 1000 hours of TV a year. If that person lives until he or she is 65 years old, they will have spent 9 ½ years watching TV. If that same person goes to church once a week they will have spent only 4 months in church. No wonder we lose sight of what is really important. What we give our time to will determine the values we have.

One day we will all face our Creator, no one really knows where or when. James 4:13-15 says, "Now listen, you who say, "Today or tomorrow we will go to this or that city, spend a year there, carry on business and make money." Why, you do not even know what will happen tomorrow. What is your life? You are a mist that appears for a little while and then vanishes. Instead, you ought to say, "If it is the Lord's will, we will live and do this or that."" In other words, we do everything on this earth planning for eternity. What is it that's really important to you? Do you want houses, cars, money, status, or just to have an easy life? None of these will ever really bring satisfaction. Only Jesus can.

I have been to two of my friends' funerals recently. They were both very sad occasions for me and for many others. However, for the believers it was not sadness filled with despair, as we know that they have both gone to be with our Saviour. In times like these you see those who have a real walk with the Lord, and those who are lukewarm. You can see it on their faces, either grief or despair. 2 Corinthians 5:8 tells us 'to be absent in the body is to be present with the Lord.' I will miss my friends, their jokes, the friendships and the fun times together but I know that one day I will see them again.

Psalm 116:15 says, 'Precious to the Lord is the death of His saints.' As believers we know that this life is only an introduction for the next, and the choices we make today will determine where we spend eternity. What do you live your life for?

So What Does This Mean To Me?

1. How Important Is Your Church Family To You?

Do you make weak excuses to miss Church? Is TV more important than Church? Are you setting a good example for your kids to follow?

That which matters the most should not be at the mercy of that which matters the least! God is building His Church! Not ministries or revival meetings, but His glorious and spotless bride. Someone once said, "If you are a lukewarm Christian, you live your life in such a way that you don't offend the devil!"

2. Are You Ready To Be With Jesus?

It may sound a bit morbid and harsh, but we should all live our life ready at any moment to be with Him. In Luke 12:13-20, Jesus talks about the rich young fool who decided to build other barns and expand his empire, but He said, "you fool; tonight your very life will be demanded of you. And what will become of all your wealth?"

3. Live Life For His Kingdom.

We all have been given the same amount of hours in a day. We will always have other things on, important things to do, but you will make time for whatever is most important to you. As my spiritual father Rev. Colin Cooper says, "A man will do what he wants to do!" Make a choice today to live for His kingdom. Give today your 4 T's to God: your Time, your Treasure, your Talent and your Touch!

Scriptures:

Joshua 23:10 (New King James Version)
One man of you shall chase a thousand, for the LORD your God is He who fights for you, as He promised you.

Galatians 2:20 (New Living Translation)
My old self has been crucified with Christ. It is no longer I who live, but Christ lives in me. So I live in this earthly body by trusting in the Son of God, who loved me and gave himself for me.

Chapter 18

His House Is Your Home

Psalm 84:4 (Amplified Bible)
Blessed (happy, fortunate, to be envied) are those who dwell in Your house and Your presence; they will be singing Your praises all the day long. Selah [pause, and calmly think of that]!

The House of the Lord should be the number one priority in our lives. In the House there is safety, rest, blessings, accountability, strength, power and encouragement. God and Church go hand in hand. In other words, to love God is to love His House - you cannot separate the two! Church was never mans' idea, it came from the very heart of God. Jesus declared this in Matthew 17:17-19, saying, "I will build my church..."

In Acts 9, Paul thought that he was doing the will of God by persecuting the Church. However, Jesus said these words to Him: "Saul, Saul why do you persecute me?" To attack the church is to attack Jesus Christ himself.

In every church there are a certain set of guidelines and Biblical principles that will be unique to that church. Those who are joined to the Church come under these specific guidelines and principles, as they not only partner with the Church, but also come under the leadership of that local House (see Hebrews 13:17).

Acts 2:42
"They devoted themselves to the apostles' teaching and to fellowship, to the breaking of bread and to prayer."

Notice the guidelines and principles: It started first with devoting yourselves to the apostles' teaching and to fellowship. They saw it fit to devote themselves to what was being taught at their local church, and to fellowship together with the breaking of bread and in prayer.

In doing this we all help build great churches that will not only influence our cities, but also bring many lost souls into the Kingdom of God.

So What Does This Mean To Me?

1. I Listen To The Word

Romans 10:17 says, "Faith comes by hearing, and hearing by the Word of God". This is very important to your spiritual growth in God.

Be in church every time the church doors open! Getting the Word in you should be your number one goal. Just as we hunger if we miss a meal, we should hunger for the Word of God. Today we have the Word so readily available to us, take advantage of it and grow.

2. I Don't Miss Church

Hebrews 10:25 says, "Let us not give up meeting together, as some are in the habit of doing, but let us encourage one another - and all the more as you see the Day approaching."

It's very easy these days, in the midst of a busy life, to miss church. But the warning from Hebrews is very clear, 'Let us not give up meeting together…' Think about the reasons why you miss Church. It's not enough to attend Church only on a Sunday. Get involved like the saints in Acts 2 did; meeting together, breaking bread and sharing fellowship with those of the same mind and spirit.

3. I Guard My Heart

1 Corinthians 5:11 warns about people we should not associate with; those who walk out of the fellowship and covering of your local church. They will have various reasons, but the Bible says in this and many other scriptures, 'have nothing to do with them'. You will poison and severely hinder your walk with God if you continue to fellowship with such people. Notice that in Acts 2:42 the fellowship was with those who 'continue in the apostles' doctrine.' Many may find this a very difficult thing, however, if you look at Matthew 18:15-17, people who choose to be offended (offence is a choice!) and continue to walk in offence should be avoided! Why? Eventually that poison will take effect in you!

Scripture:

Acts 2:42-45 (New Living Translation)
[42]All the believers devoted themselves to the apostles' teaching, and to fellowship, and to sharing in meals (including the Lord's Supper), and to prayer. [43]A deep sense of awe came over them all, and the apostles performed many miraculous signs and wonders. [44]And all the believers met together in one place and shared everything they had. [45]They sold their property and possessions and shared the money with those in need.

Section 3

Me

.

Chapter 19

Watch Your Steps!

Romans 8:1 (New King James Version)
There is therefore now no condemnation to those who are in Christ Jesus, who do not walk according to the flesh, but according to the Spirit.

Watching our children take their first steps is amazing, exciting and emotional. Our Christian life can be the same way; when we give our lives to Jesus, we have some first steps to take. Often in those first couple of weeks we will stumble and fall, but by the grace of God we are able to stand. One of the things that keep us from getting up can be condemnation; it can come in unbeknownst to anyone else but you. You can feel it during services, even when there is a great presence of God, and joy and laughter are all around you. How do we fight against that feeling? *Anyone* can all suffer from the feeling of being inadequate and under-equipped to do what God asks of us.

The Apostle Paul tells us:

Galatians 2:20 (New Living Translation):
"My old self has been crucified with Christ. It is no longer I who live, but Christ lives in me. So I live in this earthly body by trusting in the Son of God, who loved me and gave himself for me."

The Christian life is all about exchange; exchanging all we are for all He is. The only way to overcome condemnation is to develop a personal walk with the Holy

Spirit. Jesus sent the Holy Spirit as a guide, a comforter and a helper (John 14:15-31). As a newborn believer or even a mature Christian, each one of us needs a *personal* relationship with the Holy Spirit in our lives. We overcome fleshly vices by the Holy Spirit, and if we walk according to the prompting of the Spirit we will not be ruled by our emotions or fleshly desires (Galatians 5:16-26).

The challenge is not to pray for another revival, or pray for another move of God. The challenge is for each one of us to watch our steps and walk in total obedience to God's Word. If we do that then we will have no condemnation in our lives.

So What Does This Mean To Me?

1. My Past is My Past

Don't let what you have done stop you from doing what God wants you to do. Our past will often try and remind us of what we cannot do, but once we are in Christ we are a new creation. New creation means exactly that - new! Not 'approved used' or 'reconditioned', but new! (2 Corinthians 5:17; 1 John 4:4).

2. God Never Condemns You!

The Holy Spirit was sent to convict the world of sin. Conviction is totally different to condemnation. The devil is known as the one who condemns us, and tries to stop us by saying "there's no way out". Jesus however came as 'The Way, the Truth and the Life'. He provides access when all other doors seem to be closed, when there seems to be 'no other way.' Jesus will never leave you, nor will He condemn you. He will deal with blatant sin and punish the wicked, but not those who are truly repentant and being changed from glory to glory (John 3:16-17; John 14:6; Acts 2:38).

3. The Church Is Where I Get Strength and Encouragement

One of the destructive tendencies of believers is to miss church during a tough time or season. The church is God's instrument of change on the earth. That change only happens as our lives are transformed and we are given strength in times of weakness. Church should be the number one place to be, especially when things seem to overwhelm us and we feel we cannot handle it anymore. Often, during worship or the preached Word, God will minister to us and help us at our very point of need. To miss church is to miss our moment to be changed and strengthened and for God to work on our behalf (Micah 1:1-2; Hebrews 10:25; Ephesians 2:19-22; 4:11-16).

Scripture:

Hebrews 12:1 (New King James Version)
Therefore we also, since we are surrounded by so great a cloud of witnesses, let us lay aside every weight, and the sin which so easily ensnares us, and let us run with endurance the race that is set before us.

Chapter 20

Great Marriages

Ephesians 5:21-25 (New Living Translation) - Wives and Husbands
And further, submit to one another out of reverence for Christ. For wives, this means submit to your husbands as to the Lord. For a husband is the head of his wife as Christ is the head of the church. He is the Saviour of his body, the church. As the church submits to Christ, so you wives should submit to your husbands in everything. For husbands, this means love your wives, just as Christ loved the church. He gave up his life for her.

Godly relationships can be the most beautiful thing to watch. The Bible tells us in Psalm 133 that where unity exists, God commands blessings on that relationship. When it comes to husband and wife relationships the Bible is very clear. "Wives submit to your husbands." "Husbands love your wife as Christ loves the Church."

Men are called to provide godly leadership in the home and marriage. This includes all things spiritual as well as everyday matters. Men are to be the head and provide godly and graceful leadership, like Christ. Our pattern is not another man or couple, but Christ as a standard. What did Christ do? He loved the Church so much that He laid down His life for her.

Women are called to submit to their husbands' leadership and his example as he follows Christ. Women are not to be divisive or manipulative, they are not to cry or even withhold marital duties in order to sway a situation her way.

1 Corinthians 7:1-6 says that the body of the wife belongs to her husband and the husband's body to the wife.

In the age in which we live, this may seem restrictive and old fashioned. However, it is not. When the husband and wife work as a team in unity and understanding of each other's roles, God himself commands blessings on that relationship. Marriage should be a joy and not a burden. It should last a lifetime and not just a moment. Put God in the centre and submit to one another and watch how God will bless your marriage.

What Does This Mean To Me?

1. Wives Submit To Your Husbands

There's nothing worse than a nagging wife. Proverbs likens it to a 'dripping tap.' Wives honour your husbands. Become a helpmate to him, encourage him, and provide a good atmosphere for him and your children to come home to. A man will often be attracted to someone who encourages him. Wives, be an encouragement to your man.

2. Husbands Love Your Wives

Paul uses these words, "love your wives as Christ loves the Church!" This may seem 'unfair' as Christ gave His life for the Church, but men are commanded to do the same. Don't speak negatively about your wife. Praise her with your lips and say good things about her to others. Go the extra mile to make your wife feel loved. Be spontaneous, fun, and take her out!

3. Keep Christ In The Centre

Let your relationships be covered by Christ. Let church be the centre of your marriage, your home and your family. Raise the standard in your home, so your children can be taught godly values.

Scriptures:

Ephesians 4:32 (New Living Translation)
Instead, be kind to each other, tender-hearted, forgiving one another, just as God through Christ has forgiven you.

1 Peter 3:1-7 (New Living Translation)

Wives
¹In the same way, you wives must accept the authority of your husbands. Then, even if some refuse to obey the Good News, your godly lives will speak to them without any words. They will be won over ²by observing your pure and reverent lives.

³Don't be concerned about the outward beauty of fancy hairstyles, expensive jewellery, or beautiful clothes. ⁴You should clothe yourselves instead with the beauty that comes from within, the unfading beauty of a gentle and quiet spirit, which is so precious to God. ⁵This is how the holy women of old made themselves beautiful. They trusted God and accepted the authority of their husbands. ⁶For instance, Sarah obeyed her husband, Abraham, and called him her master. You are her daughters when you do what is right without fear of what your husbands might do.

Husbands
⁷In the same way, you husbands must give honour to your wives. Treat your wife with understanding as you live together. She may be weaker than you are, but she is your equal partner in God's gift of new life. Treat her as you should so your prayers will not be hindered.

Chapter 21

Chat With Your Kids

Psalm 78:5-7 (New Living Translation)
5For he issued his laws to Jacob; he gave his instructions to Israel. He commanded our ancestors to teach them to their children, 6so the next generation might know them—even the children not yet born—and they in turn will teach their own children. 7So each generation should set its hope anew on God, not forgetting his glorious miracles and obeying his commands.

I love my relationship with my sons, they both bring so much joy to my life it's unbelievable. Kids can say the funniest things: I was once telling my son why Daddy had a scar on his arm, as when I was young man in Trinidad and Tobago I was kidnapped and cut with a machete. I was telling him how God saved me from what could have been certain death. Then my other son came running in the room with something he thought was exciting and butted into our conversation, to the horror of my first son who just said, "Shut Up! Daddy is talking about the miracle of how God saved him from being hacked to pieces!" Of course an argument broke out which I had to stop and then I later finished the story.

It's important that we pass onto to the next generation what the Lord has done. So often we can get so busy with work, or even church and conferences, that we forget to share with those little ones the miracles and wonders God does or has done for us. Joshua is a personal hero of mine, but the wonderful things he did are overshadowed by his failure to pass them down to the next generation

Chip Kawalsingh

(Judges 2:10; Joel 1:3). A good practice is to sit down and eat together as a family. Don't eat in front of the TV, but take time to 'Hear and Share.' Talk with your kids about their day or week. Ask them how they handle any tough situations, encouraging them with positive, uplifting words.

Kids will often learn by watching you! They watch not only what you say, but also what you do! They look at how you deal with tough situations. Kids are very good at spotting when there is one rule for them and another for you. Remember to let your yes be yes! And pass onto the next generation the wonders of our God, and see this generation set their hope in God anew.

My Action Plan:

1. Spend Time With Your Kids

There is a myth that we must spend 'quality time' with our kids. Anytime with your kids, during which they get your undivided attention, *is* quality time. You don't really need to make extensive plans, just plan to spend time together. Kids learn and benefit from just being with you, whatever you are doing.

2. Don't Take Them Out Of Church

Taking your child out of church to spend time with them is not a wise thing to do. The Church is God's plan to bring about change on the earth through our lives, so having them in church is the best thing you can do. Make sure they are there, no matter what. It's part of the training-up period which means it must be enforced over and over again (Proverbs 22:3).

3. Use Encouraging Words

Kids can sometimes drive you crazy! And it seems that you can spend weeks just 'telling them off' or disciplining them. It's a good practice, however, to balance how you use your words. Discipline is very important, but so is encouragement. Don't fall into the trap of comparing your kids with others.

They are unique and God's gift to you. Treat them with respect and use positive words to reinforce confidence in them. Kids are like arrows in the hands of a warrior, don't cause these weapons to be turned on you through constant negative words and actions. It's sad to think that some kids grow to be adults not hearing the words "I love you!"

Scriptures:

Psalm 127:3-5 (The Message)
Don't you see that children are GOD's best gift? The fruit of the womb his generous legacy? Like a warrior's fistful of arrows are the children of a vigorous youth. Oh, how blessed are you parents with your quivers full of children! Your enemies don't stand a chance against you; you'll sweep them right off your doorstep.

Colossians 3:21 (Contemporary English Version)
Parents, don't be hard on your children. If you are, they might give up.

Chapter 22

Master Your Life, Or It Will Master You!

Proverbs 17:24 (Amplified Bible)
A man of understanding sets skilful and godly Wisdom before his face, but the eyes of a [self-confident] fool are on the ends of the earth.

Have you ever come to the end of your day and thought, "Did I get anything done today?" Where does all the time go? The more I do, it seems the less is done! I often think that God only extends the efforts of things I do when I give Him the best of my time *first*. The first and the best always belong to God. If not, we will never seem to be effective or fruitful as leaders, employees, or in any of our other roles.

Leadership is about leading others, but it starts with our own lives first. You cannot give out of what you don't have. Fill your cup first, help yourself and only then will you be able to help others. God cannot use you if you're spiritually dead! This is driven home to me every time I fly. The cabin crew will go through the safety briefing, saying, "If the cabin loses pressure the oxygen masks will drop. Put your own mask on first before helping anyone else!" If you don't do it that way, then both people risk losing their lives. In the same way, if you don't master your schedule, it will master you.

Chip Kawalsingh

So What Does This Mean To Me?

Here are three suggestions from the Bible for reducing the stress of your to-do list:

1. Get Your Priorities Right

Obviously, you don't have time to do everything. You must make choices. You must decide what's really important and what isn't. Take some time to consider the direction of your life.

Proverbs 12:11 (Today's English Version)
"It is stupid to waste time on useless projects."

Proverbs 16:9 (Today's English Version)
"You may make your plans, but God directs your actions."

2. Change Your Thinking

Stinking thinking will affect your attitude. Do you really have to do everything on your to-do list? A lot of your stress can often be self-imposed. You can run yourself ragged taking kids to football, karate, swimming or cricket. Your life becomes like that old Beatles song, *Here, There and Everywhere*. The Bible says that God gave us humour as a stress reliever. Slow down and enjoy a good laugh with a spouse, friend or family member.

Proverbs 12:25 (New Living Translation)
"Worry weighs a person down; an encouraging word cheers a person up."

Proverbs 14:30 (New Living Translation)
"A relaxed attitude lengthens life; jealousy rots it away."

Proverbs 17:22 (New Living Translation)
"A cheerful heart is good medicine, but a broken spirit saps a person's strength."

3. Daily focus on Jesus.

Stress can often be a warning light. We may have taken our focus off God and are looking at our problems from our own limited viewpoint. One of the greatest dangers to believers today is that we take our eyes off Jesus and begin to do things in our own strength, training or gifting. **Stop!** Take your eyes off the mountain of "to-do's" and look to the Lord, for that is where your strength comes from.

Scriptures:

Proverbs 10:27 (New Living Translation)
"Fear of the Lord lengthens one's life, but the years of the wicked are cut short."

Proverbs 14:26 (New Living Translation)
"Those who fear the Lord are secure; he will be a place of refuge for their children."

Chapter 23

Fruitful Work Versus Fruitless Toil

Luke 5:5 (The Message)

Simon said, "Master, we've been fishing hard all night and haven't caught even a minnow. But if you say so, I'll let out the nets."
It was no sooner said than done—a huge haul of fish, straining the nets past capacity. They waved to their partners in the other boat to come help them. They filled both boats, nearly swamping them with the catch.

Fishing is close to my heart, as anyone who has met me will know. I understand about fruitless nights and even days of being at sea and catching nothing, so when Peter said "we've been fishing hard all night and caught nothing" I understood. Simon Peter was a professional fisherman, making his living from fishing. He knew where to go, he knew the tides, the moon, the hot spots and still nothing worked! Peter did two amazing things. Firstly, he obeyed Jesus, saying, "If you say so, I'll let out the nets." Because of choosing to obey God rather than following his experience, training or knowledge, the result was success. Secondly, at the end of this passage, they left it all and followed Jesus.

Chip Kawalsingh

So What Does This Mean To Me?

1. We Are To Obey His Voice Over Our Experiences And Emotions

I Samuel 15:22 tells us that "to obey is better than sacrifice." In other words, get to know His voice and obey it. God speaks through different vessels. He can use parents, teachers, pastors, situations, or even an unbeliever to speak to us. The key is to recognize His voice through the Holy Spirit. The disciples couldn't rely on emotions and past experiences - they had tried and caught nothing after fishing all night! But at His word, they obeyed.

2. Hard Work Without Jesus In The Boat Is Hard Work And Unfulfilling

Simon Peter had Jesus with him: 1 John 4:4, "the one who is in you is greater than the one who is in the world." It's easy to get tired, stressed and weary from hard work - I know it myself! But I have learnt that the secret to staying strong is found in my daily devotions with God. Isaiah 40:31 says, "But those who hope in the LORD will renew their strength. They will soar on wings like eagles; they will run and not grow weary, they will walk and not be faint." Are you feeling over-tired or stressed out? How's your daily walk with the Lord?

3. Jesus Brings Fulfillment, Not The Fish!

Simon Peter had learnt a lesson. Jesus brings the fulfillment, not the fish. We can focus on our jobs, position and what we do to bring fulfillment, and for a while it may make us 'feel good.' However, no matter what we do, who we are, or how much we do for Jesus, it does not compare to just being with Him. Luke 10:40 says Martha was distracted by all that she was doing, which was not a bad thing in itself, but she forgot to sit at Jesus' feet. When was the last time you stopped what you were doing, shut everything else off, and sat at His feet?

4. It Takes Relationships To Help With The Harvest

Lastly, to help with the harvest will take sacrifice, commitment and relationships. For Church to work anywhere, these are three pivotal ingredients. It is not just counting the fish in the net, but helping with those in the boat. Open your circle of friendships, don't just sit with the same group during and after services, but open the circle and make room for the 'new fish.' Whenever we get blessed with new souls in our churches, it's not just enough to say, "Well, they are in!" No, we must now go on to make them disciples. Take time to get to know them. Invite them round, and let's prepare for more harvest.

Scriptures:

Matthew 28:19-20 (New King James Version)
[19]Go therefore and make disciples of all the nations, baptizing them in the name of the Father and of the Son and of the Holy Spirit, [20]teaching them to observe all things that I have commanded you; and lo, I am with you always, even to the end of the age." Amen.

Acts 2:42-47 (The Message)
[42]That day about three thousand took him at his word, were baptized and were signed up. They committed themselves to the teaching of the apostles, the life together, the common meal, and the prayers. [43-45]Everyone around was in awe—all those wonders and signs done through the apostles! And all the believers lived in a wonderful harmony, holding everything in common. They sold whatever they owned and pooled their resources so that each person's need was met. [46-47]They followed a daily discipline of worship in the Temple followed by meals at home, every meal a celebration, exuberant and joyful, as they praised God. People in general liked what they saw. Every day their number grew as God added those who were saved.

Chapter 24

Do Everything Without Grumbling!

Philippians 2:12-14 (Contemporary English Version)
[12]My dear friends, you always obeyed when I was with you. Now that I am away, you should obey even more. So work with fear and trembling to discover what it really means to be saved. [13]God is working in you to make you willing and able to obey him. [14]Do everything without grumbling or arguing.

As Christians, we should be some of the most happy, joyful and pleasant people to be with on the whole earth. We should be people without bad attitudes, people without offences and people who see everything in the light of eternity and of what Jesus did on the cross. Often there is a huge gap between what we know and what we do!

What we do for God and His Kingdom is not always going to be easy. It will cause stresses, require sacrifices and may bring some hardship. This is why Paul said in Philippians 3:13-14 (paraphrase) "One thing I do, forgetting what is behind and straining toward what is ahead, I press on..." The Christian life is a marathon and not a 100 metre sprint. It's a long-term race, not without trials, testing and hardships - these are all part of the normal Christian life. In 2 Corinthians 4:16-18, Paul asks his readers "not to lose heart", and then goes on to tell them that their momentary problems are achieving for them an eternal glory that far outweighs every trouble we have or will ever face. The answer, he says, lies in what you fix your eyes on! Do you focus on your problems, your needs and your wants? Or do you focus on Jesus?

Jesus himself tells us in John 16:33 "In this world you will have trouble, but take heart, I (Jesus) have overcome the world!" How are we to face such trials and hardships? With faith in God! James 1: 2-4 tells us it should be counted pure joy! Our joy is not for the troubles, but because we know that as we overcome each one without grumbling or complaining James says we will be "mature and complete, lacking nothing!"

Most believers today grumble and complain about things that are really not worth the breath. When I was a child, I grew up in Trinidad with my brothers and parents. My father (who was a full time pastor then) always made us give thanks for everything we had, whether we liked to or not! I remember a song we used to sing in our church back in the West Indies "Count your blessings, name them one by one, count your many blessings and see what God has done!"

Let's cease grumbling and complaining and stop for a moment and thank God for what we have and for what he has done! (Whether you feel like it or not!)

Things to Remember:

1. Guard Against Negative Talk

No one likes being around a negative person, much less being married to one! Words are very important, they represent life! Proverbs 18:21 tells us that "life and death is in the power of the tongue!" Are you a life-giver or do you bring death with your words? Ask the Holy Spirit to help you with your words.

2. Guard Your Heart

Proverbs 4:23 says "Above all else, guard your heart!" This proverb can be a lifesaver; offences and bitterness can lodge themselves in your heart and affect your outlook and your course in life. Let your heart always remain pure by being quick to forgive. Remember, offence is a choice: "Choose not to get offended!"

3. Guard Your Friendships

Unfortunately, the people who tend to suffer the most when we are negative and bitter are those who are closest to us. We should always keep a short account with each other and build each other up in the faith. Why not ask people around for a time of fellowship and let us build the Kingdom of God together by being the happiest, greatest people with the best attitudes on the planet!

Scriptures:

Proverbs 12:26 (New Living Translation)
The godly give good advice to their friends; the wicked lead them astray.

Proverbs 16:28 (New Living Translation)
A troublemaker plants seeds of strife; gossip separates the best of friends.

Chapter 25
Attitude Determines Destiny

Ephesians 4:23 (New Living Translation)
Instead, let the Spirit renew your thoughts and attitudes.

Your attitude is very important. A great attitude is not only a healthy thing, but it will also get you a long way in life. Without a great attitude, our world view becomes bleak and such a person does not make for good company. We are encouraged by Scripture to have the same attitude as Christ Jesus (Philippians 2:5).

Here are eight great life attitudes to have:

1. Have a Christ-like attitude.
2. Have the attitude of a starter.
3. Have the attitude of a finisher.
4. Have the attitude of a Church-builder.
5. Have the attitude of a giver.
6. Have an attitude of joy in every situation.
7. Have a 'trusting in God' attitude.
8. Have a 'love for God above everything else' attitude.

One of the great attitude stories in the Bible is found in Mark 10:46-52. The story is of a blind man called Bartimaeus. As you read the account, you get the impression that this man was in a desperate situation, not knowing what to do to get out of his problem. He would have heard of the man Jesus, knowing that if anyone could help, Jesus could. However, he didn't get the support of the people with him, the crowd, or even the disciples. But that didn't break his spirit: the Scripture says in verse 48, "Many rebuked him and told him to be quiet, but he shouted all the more!"

You cannot let the crowd or your culture tell you who you are and what you will do and say. No matter what sort of start you've had in life, where you're going is more important than where you come from. You've got to remember to shout all the more, cry out to God and seek Him. Trust Him!

Winston Churchill, one of Britain's greatest Prime Ministers, once said in the face of attack from the enemy "We will never surrender!" What a great attitude to have when it comes to the things of God.

So What Does This Mean To Me?

1. Pray First, Act Later

I will go to God first in every situation. Not depending on yesterday's answers to solve today's problems, I will seek God daily for a fresh word. I will break through to a higher level in God. I will hide myself in the secret place until an answer comes.

2. I Will Go To Church

I will commit myself to attend Church at all times! If it's a matter of choice, I will always choose Church over everything else. My love for God is shown in my commitment to His bride, the Church. I will not forsake the meeting together of my true family. I will talk positively about His bride, and never walk out on my Church family.

3. I Will Obey My Leaders

I will commit myself to Church and submit to God's authority in His house. To reject God's authority is to reject God! (Numbers 12: 1-11) I understand that this has nothing to do with my likes, my leaders' age, or cultural background. I obey those who have rule over me as this will bring a blessing and protection in my life. I choose to surround myself with faith people and those who are part of the local family of God.

Scriptures:

Hebrews 13:17 (Amplified Bible)
Obey your spiritual leaders and submit to them [continually recognizing their authority over you], for they are constantly keeping watch over your souls and guarding your spiritual welfare, as men who will have to render an account [of their trust]. [Do your part to] let them do this with gladness and not with sighing and groaning, for that would not be profitable to you [either].

Hebrews 10:25 (New Living Translation)
And let us not neglect our meeting together, as some people do, but encourage one another, especially now that the day of his return is drawing near.

Chapter 26

No Turning Back!

John 6:68-69 (The Message)
'Peter replied, "Master, to whom would we go? You have the words of real life, eternal life. We've already committed ourselves, confident that you are the Holy One of God."'

John 6:60-70 makes for encouraging reading, especially for those who are called to pastor. No matter how much you do, people will still walk out on you, even some who called themselves disciples. People can be shallow, act selfishly and even undermine you when all the while you have nothing but good plans and intentions for them. As I read this scripture, I wonder if Jesus felt the same way. Those disciples hearing him teach said to each other, "This is hard teaching. Who can accept it?" Later on in verse 66 the Bible says "many of His disciples turned back and no longer followed him." Jesus then turned to the Twelve and said "Do you want to leave as well?"

You see, people will follow you for a while if they feel blessed, if they can preach what they want and if they can see great things happening, but very few will stick with you through the tough times and never turn back.

Jesus felt this emotion himself. It hurts down to the gut, makes you feel low and makes you want to pack it all in. However, we can take encouragement from the faithful friends around us, who are far from perfect, but are loyal.

Chip Kawalsingh

Peter was a guy who had lots of flaws and made a lot of mistakes in his life. He said the wrong things and even denied Jesus; but when asked the question by Jesus "Do you want to leave as well?" Peter said some words that I am sure moved Jesus. In modern day language it would go something like this:

"Lord, who else or what else can I turn to? I've given up my fishing business because your words are enough for me, they feed me when I am deep in sorrow, and they put hope in my spirit. I am totally committed to you, I am convinced that you are God and there's nothing that can change that."

The Apostle Paul puts it this way:

Romans 8:35-39 (New Living Translation):
"Can anything ever separate us from Christ's love? Does it mean he no longer loves us if we have trouble or calamity, or are persecuted, or hungry, or destitute, or in danger, or threatened with death? (As the Scriptures say, "For your sake we are killed every day; we are being slaughtered like sheep.")
"No, despite all these things, overwhelming victory is ours through Christ, who loved us. And I am convinced that nothing can ever separate us from God's love. Neither death nor life, neither angels nor demons, neither our fears for today nor our worries about tomorrow—not even the powers of hell can separate us from God's love. No power in the sky above or in the earth below— indeed, nothing in all creation will ever be able to separate us from the love of God that is revealed in Christ Jesus our Lord."

My 'To-Do' List:

1. Put Your Hope in God

The greatest thing you can do in tough seasons is to put your trust in God. Mark 11:22 "Have Faith in God." He is always with us, He will never let us down. Nothing impresses Him. There is no need to try and impress Him with all you've done and achieved; as the old hymn goes, "Just as I am without one plea." He wants you just as you are.

2. Keep Your Eyes Fixed On The Eternal

With all that's happening in our world today, the best thing we can all do is focus on Jesus. Trust Him and keep our focus on Him. How do we do that? Read your Bible, pray every day, and make church a priority. When it seems that everyone else is running to a big name, a TV evangelist, a so called revival or a trend, stick in church. Trust God and watch how blessings will come your way.

3. Encouragement Always Defuses Discouragement

Although the world claims to have all the answers through technology and scientific advances, we still see so many people depressed, disillusioned and discouraged. One of the ways we deal with this is by trying to encourage someone else. Help make their dreams come true, be a friend and a help to them without looking for anything in return. As you do this, watch and see how your problems float away. You see, as we love others and help them in their time of need, God blesses us.

Scripture:

Galatians 6:9 (Contemporary English Version)
Don't get tired of helping others. You will be rewarded when the time is right, if you don't give up.

Chapter 27

Who Am I?

Galatians 2:20 (New Living Translation)
My old self has been crucified with Christ. It is no longer I who live, but Christ
lives in me. So I live in this earthly body by trusting in the Son of God, who
loved me and gave himself for me.

We live in a world where a person's identity can be stolen and misused without
their knowledge. Identity theft is on the increase, and I think we can see the
same thing in our Christian lives today. We can be the victim of someone (the
devil) using our old identity to tell us who we are. We must remember that we
are not our former selves but as believers we are new creations in Christ. You
are a new person and what really counts is this new life you live in him and
nothing else (Galatians 6:15).

2 Corinthians 5:17 (Contemporary English Version)
*Anyone who belongs to Christ is a new person. The past is forgotten, and
everything is new.*

As we celebrate and walk in this new life, we can easily forget who we really
are. Don't let that old devil tell you about your life or your true identity. We
can also hide behind religious titles and positions, our so-called good deeds
creating an image for us. The fact of the matter is that none of our righteous
deeds and good works really please God; however, obedience to Him does!

Have you ever lost something really important? Do you feel as though your right arm is missing until you find it? Well, you can never really be all that God has called you to be if you don't know who you are. Look at the life ahead of you and focus on God, not where you came from. The reason that car manufacturers make cars with a huge windscreen and a small rear-view mirror is simple; where you're going is far more important than where you just came from. Keep this same perspective in life and you will go far!

What Shall I Do?

1. Read My Bible Every Day

When you read the Word, not only will it help you but it will also help create a picture of who you are in Jesus and what He thinks about you. The devil can take days of victory and deflate them by bringing little problems that ruin your day. We should live our lives by the Word (Luke 4: 1-13).

2. Pray Everyday

When we pray we connect to God. It's the mortal talking with the immortal, it is life-giving to pray and spend time with Him. When we pray we get to know the master's voice. When we learn to recognise His voice then we can distinguish it from all other voices that can tell us otherwise (John 10:27).

3. Walk In The Spirit

Walking in the Spirit (or keeping step with the Spirit) will help form your identity. The Holy Spirit is our guide, our comforter, our source and our power. His help is all we need to overcome fleshly deeds. We are stronger when we are in tune with the Spirit.

Scriptures:

John 10:4 (The Message) - He Calls His Sheep by Name
1-5"Let me set this before you as plainly as I can. If a person climbs over or through the fence of a sheep pen instead of going through the gate, you know he's up to no good—a sheep rustler! The shepherd walks right up to the gate. The gatekeeper opens the gate to him and the sheep recognize his voice. He calls his own sheep by name and leads them out. When he gets them all out, he leads them and they follow because they are familiar with his voice. They won't follow a stranger's voice but will scatter because they aren't used to the sound of it."

Galatians 5:25 (Amplified Bible)
If we live by the [Holy] Spirit, let us also walk by the Spirit. [If by the Holy Spirit we have our life in God, let us go forward walking in line, our conduct controlled by the Spirit.

Also By Chip Kawalsingh...

In order to live a fulfilled life it will take fruitfulness. In John 15: 1-12, Jesus gives us the keys to fruitfulness, happiness and fulfilment. With these keys in our hands we are able to unlock doors, realise our destinies and reshape our lives. Join Pastors Chip and Sarah as they teach these principles through God's word. Fruitfulness awaits!

2 Corinthians 5:7 tells us that 'we live by faith, not by sight.' God wants us to focus our eyes on Him and His goodness, remembering that His promises are 'yes and Amen!' Pastor Chip challenges us in the area of obedience to God's Word in order that our faith will grow - from little faith to extravagant faith!

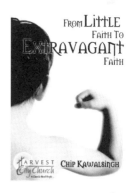

Pastor Chip often says 'The thing about common sense is that it is no longer common!' Christians today can be so spiritual, so godly and so full of Bible knowledge, yet they seem to make the same bad choices in life they always have! Join Pastors Chip and Sarah Kawalsingh as they teach what it means to make great life choices.

For more information on these materials, as well as many others, please visit

www.harvestcitypublishing.com

Also By Chip Kawalsingh...

The Partnership Guide was written by Pastor Chip Kawalsingh as a membership course for Harvest City Church. However, because of its timeless truths and principles, this book can be used for new converts as well as young leadership training sessions in any country. Harvest City Church has experienced steady and impressive growth thanks to the lessons taught in this book. An absolute must read for anyone who wants to know what church is, why it is important, and how to build a successful one!

Building and maintaining a great team is no easy task. Formation Leadership comprises a series of seminars where the heart and spiritual DNA of the senior pastors can be transferred to those who are called to leadership. Leaders need to be developed in their understanding of the 'how to' of church life. This book provides the answers, along with the attitudes, that anyone can use to springboard their leadership team into formation.

For more information on these materials, as well as many others, please visit

www.harvestcitypublishing.com